To my sunsh
continue dreaming big dreams,
reaching new heights, and inspiring
those around you.

Hi everyone, Charlie and Ada here, excited to journey with you through the ABCs of Computer Science.

As you travel through the letters, you will learn so much and be ready to take on the world of computer science in a whole new way.

BINARY

A numerical system that contains zeros and ones to store, process, and transmit information within a computer

CODE

A set of instructions written for a computer to understand

ETHERNET

A wired connection used to connect a computer to a network

F
FUNCTION

A chunk of code that performs a single task that can be used over and over again

G
GRAPHICS INTERCHANGEABLE FORMAT (GIF)

A file type for animated images

INTERNET PROTOCOL (IP) ADDRESS

A unique address that tells the location of a device on a network

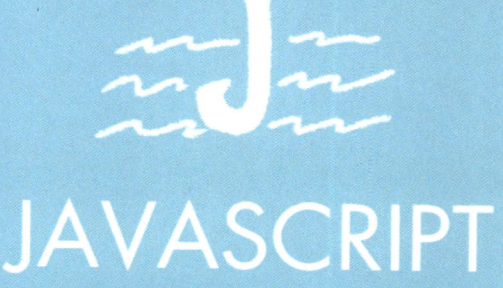

JAVASCRIPT

A programming language developed to make web pages interactive

K

KEYBOARD SHORTCUT

Two or three keys used to accomplish a digital task quickly

LOOP

A sequence of repeated instructions to complete a task

·· M ··
MAC ADDRESS

A unique series of letters and numbers separated by colons that identifies a device's hardware

N
NETWORK

Two or more devices that share sources of data and communicate with one another

OPERATING SYSTEM

Software that communicates with the hardware of a computer and allows it to run programs

PATTERN

Parts of data that have one or more similarities

RANDOM ACCESS MEMORY (RAM)

A form of short-term computer memory

S
SOFTWARE

The programs and applications that run on computers

TROUBLESHOOTING

Trying different tasks until you find a solution to the problem

U
UNIFORM RESOURCE LOCATOR (URL)

The address to a specific website or location on the internet

V

VARIABLE

Stores a specific value within a computer's program

WI-FI

Wireless networking technology that gives devices the capability to communicate without wires

EXTENSIBLE MARKUP LANGUAGE (XML)

A standard language used to exchange data

YOU

A Computer Science expert in the making!

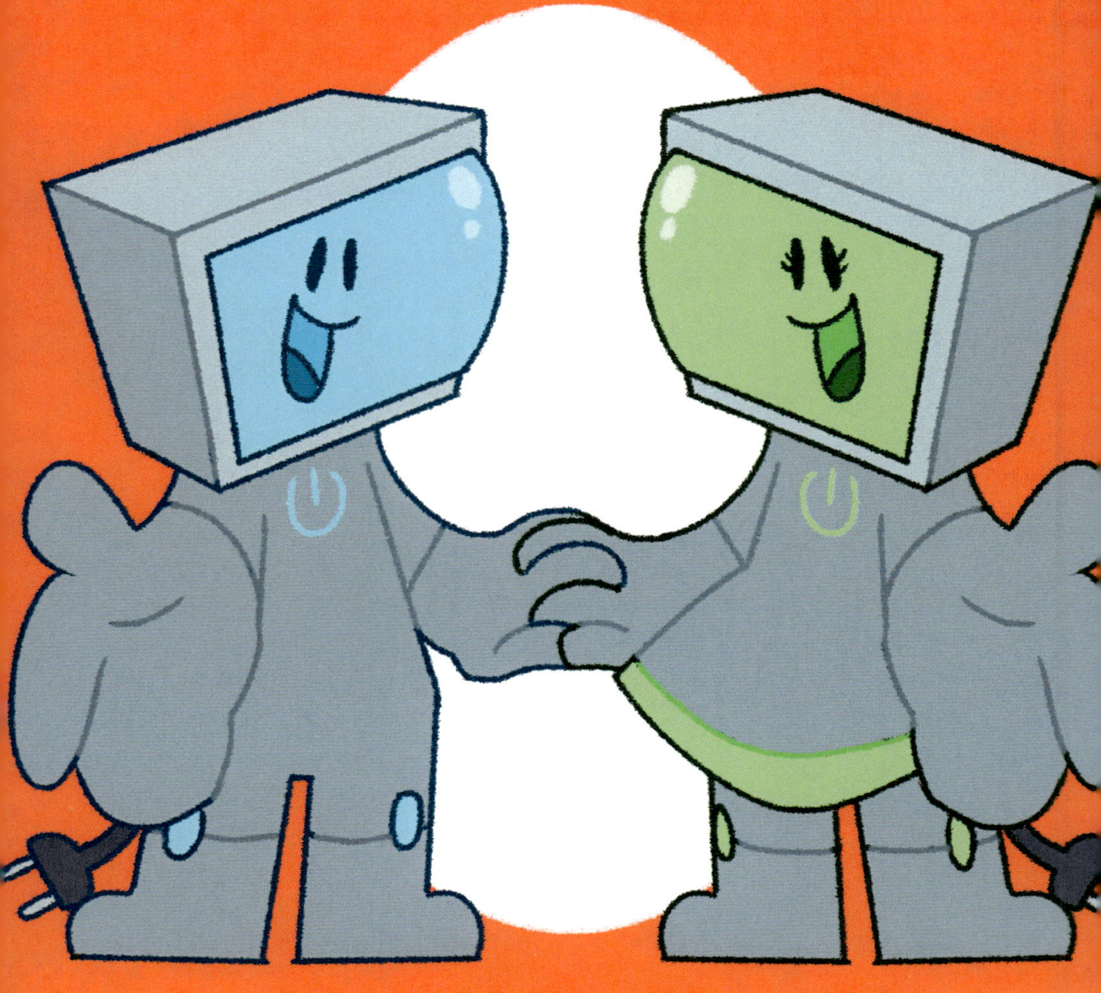

Z
ZIP FILE

A file that contains one or more files compressed to a smaller size

AUTHOR

Ashlee Elliott has been an educator for 11 years. She spent the first 9 years of her career in the elementary classroom, teaching 3rd and 4th grades. In her current role, she serves a large school district as a K-12 instructional technology coach and has a passion for preparing the younger generations for the world that lies ahead of them. Outside of education, she is a mother and wife and loves spending time with her family.

ILLUSTRATOR

Jayla Coleman is a 17-year-old high school student, approaching her senior year. It's her hope to inspire more aspiring artists with her work throughout this book. Jayla's hobbies consist of creative avocations, including varying art forms. Outside of her hobby of art, she enjoys music and writing, just to name a few.

Made in United States
Orlando, FL
08 April 2024